I Am Amazing!

A Confidence-Building Journal for Children

Ages 5-8

By

Valerie J. Lewis Coleman

Published by

Pen of the Writer, LLC
Englewood, Ohio
PenOfTheWriter.com

Published by

Pen of the Writer, LLC
Englewood, Ohio
PenOfTheWriter.com

Welcome!

This Journal Belongs to

____

This journal is a place where I can

Write

Think

Learn

Grow

Put your special sticker here

My Amazing Sticker

This journal was made just for me.

Why Your Story Matters

Your story is special because it belongs to *you*.

    The way you think.

    The way you feel.

    The things you dream about.

    The things you've been through.

    All of it matters.

Writing helps you

- Understand your feelings

- Share your ideas

- Build confidence

- Remember what makes you unique

There is no right or wrong way to use this journal. You don't have to be perfect. You don't have to know all the answers.

Just be you. Because **your voice matters**—and the world needs to hear it.

A Note for Parents, Teachers, and Facilitators

Your child is about to begin a powerful journey of self-discovery. Some pages repeat throughout the journal because young children grow through repetition. When children return to the same prompts, they often:

- Express new ideas

- Use different words

- Draw with more confidence

- See themselves in new ways

There are no right or wrong answers in this journal.

Children may:

- Write on one page and draw on another

- Use stickers some days and not others

- Skip pages and return to them later

We encourage you to:

- Read prompts aloud

- Invite conversation

- Celebrate effort, not perfection

- Allow children to respond at their own pace

Every page is an invitation for children to reflect, dream, and discover the amazing person they already are. Each time a child revisits a page, they practice something powerful—seeing themselves as capable, growing, and full of potential. Encourage your child to write freely, draw boldly, and return to these pages again and again.

Look for ★ moments—these are great opportunities to invite your child to share their thoughts with you.

About When I See Me™

When I See Me™ is a literacy and confidence-building initiative created to help children see themselves as capable, valued, and worthy of greatness. Through books, journals, book fairs, and creative experiences, children are encouraged to explore their feelings, express their ideas, and discover the power of their own voices.

Each When I See Me™ journal supports emotional growth, self-awareness, and imagination while affirming a child's identity and potential. The activities inside invite children to reflect, create, and grow in ways that feel safe, engaging, and fun.

Through the When I See Me™ Children's Book Fairs, this mission comes to life in communities—placing diverse, empowering books directly into children's hands and creating experiences where they can meet authors, engage in meaningful activities, and see themselves as readers, writers, and leaders.

At its heart, When I See Me™ is about representation, encouragement, and helping every child believe:

"I matter. My voice matters. My story matters."

Learn more at **WhenISeeMe.com.**

Now, let's jump back in—there's something special waiting for you.

Meet Your When I See Me™ Friends

Now it's your turn. Before you begin, let's meet some friends who will be on this journey with you. They're discovering who they are—just like you.

Lyric, **Shawn**, **Nia**, **Samara**, and **Zoe** are here to cheer you on. They'll help you believe in yourself, understand your feelings, and use your voice with confidence. Every day, they're learning and growing—just like you.

I'm Lyric.

I love being me and showing up with confidence and joy.

Even on the days you forget, I remind you—something special is inside you.

I am amazing just the way I am.

I'm Shawn.

I believe growth takes time, and every step matters. I keep trying, even when things feel hard.

I remind you that mistakes help you learn and grow stronger every day.

I grow and learn every day.

I'm Nia.

I help make space for big feelings and gentle moments. I take time to understand what's happening inside my heart.

I remind you that every emotion has a purpose—and it's okay to feel them all.

All my feelings are welcome.

I'm Samara.

I use my voice to share ideas, lead, and encourage others. I'm not afraid to speak up and share what's on my mind.

I remind you that your voice matters—and what you say is important.

My voice matters.

I'm Zoe.

I love stories and turning ideas into something magical. I imagine, create, and express myself in my own unique way.

I remind you that your ideas are powerful and your creativity shines brightly.

I can create my own story.

Which When I See Me™ friend are you today?

Meet Lyric

Hi! I'm Lyric. I believe you are amazing just the way you are. When you stand tall and smile big, you shine with confidence and joy. I'm here to cheer you on!

What colors will you use to show how amazing you are?

I Am Amazing Because...

Write, draw, or use a sticker to show what makes you amazing.

I am amazing because _______________________

All About Me

My name is _______________________________

I am _______________ years old.

My favorite thing to do is _______________________________

Draw yourself doing your favorite thing.

When I Feel Good

What makes you feel happy?

Show what makes you happy! Write, draw, or use a sticker.

I Can Do Hard Things

Something I learned to do:

____

____

Write, draw, or use a sticker to show how you felt.

I didn't give up!

Lyric believes in you.

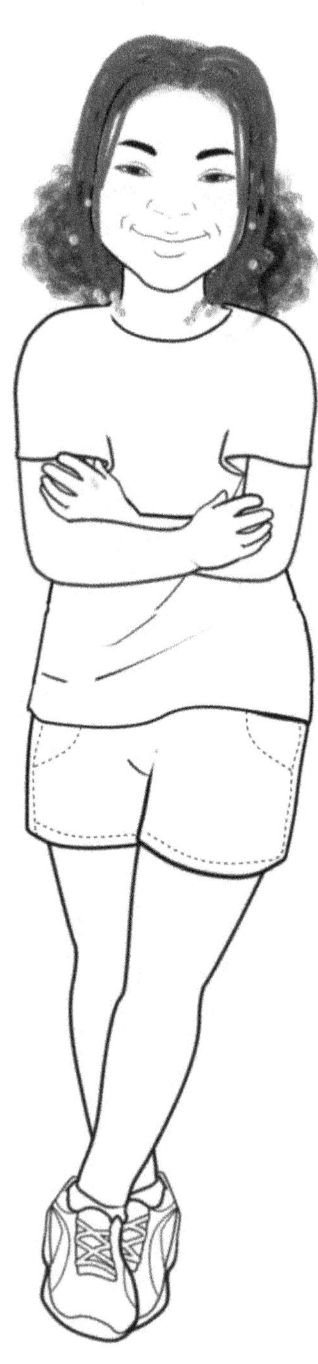

I Am Growing!

Something I'm getting better at:

____

____

Each step shows how you are growing. Draw yourself on the top step to celebrate how far you've come.

You may add a sticker that shows how you feel as you grow.

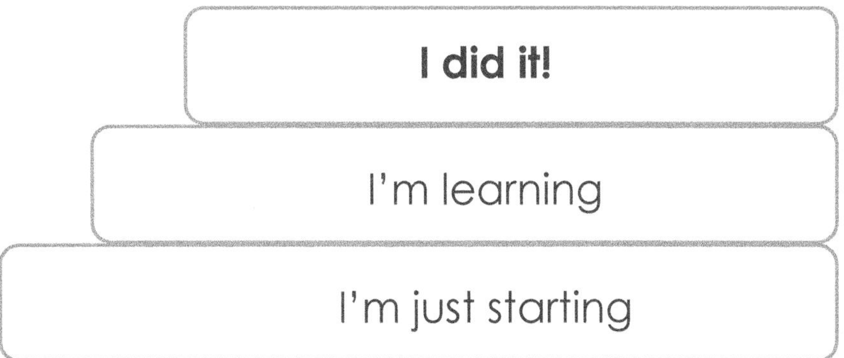

Kind Words About Me

These are kind words I can say about myself:

I am kind.

I am smart.

I am strong.

Say these words out loud.
You may trace them if you want.
How do they make you feel?

____

One more kind word about me is

____

You may add a sticker that reminds you of how special you are.

You Are Amazing!

Draw yourself doing something amazing.

This is me being amazing because

⭐ *Tell someone about this page.*

Someone I Helped

I helped someone when

____

____

Draw that moment.

People Who Matter to Me

Someone who helps take care of me ________________________

Someone I like to play with ________________________

Someone who makes me smile ________________________

Draw you and someone you love.

When I Feel Good

What makes you feel happy?

Show what makes you happy! Write, draw, or use a sticker.

I Kept Going!

Something that was hard, but I kept trying:

____

____

What helped me keep going?

____

____

Draw yourself not giving up.

Take a break and color with Lyric.

I Am Growing!

I'm getting better at:

____

____

Each step shows how you are growing. Draw yourself on the top step to celebrate how far you've come.

You may add a sticker that shows how you feel as you grow.

Kind Words About Me

These are kind words I can say about myself:

I am brave.

I am capable.

I am important.

Say these words out loud.
You may trace them if you want.
How do they make you feel?

____

One more kind word about me is

____

You may add a sticker that reminds you of how special you are.

One Thing I Love About Me

Draw something you love about yourself.

One thing I love about me is

____

____

____

⭐ *Tell someone what you love about yourself.*

My Feelings Today

Today I feel ____

When I feel this way, I like to ______________________________

____

____

Write, draw, or use a sticker to show how you feel.

I Am Amazing Because...

Write, draw, or use a sticker that shows what makes you amazing.

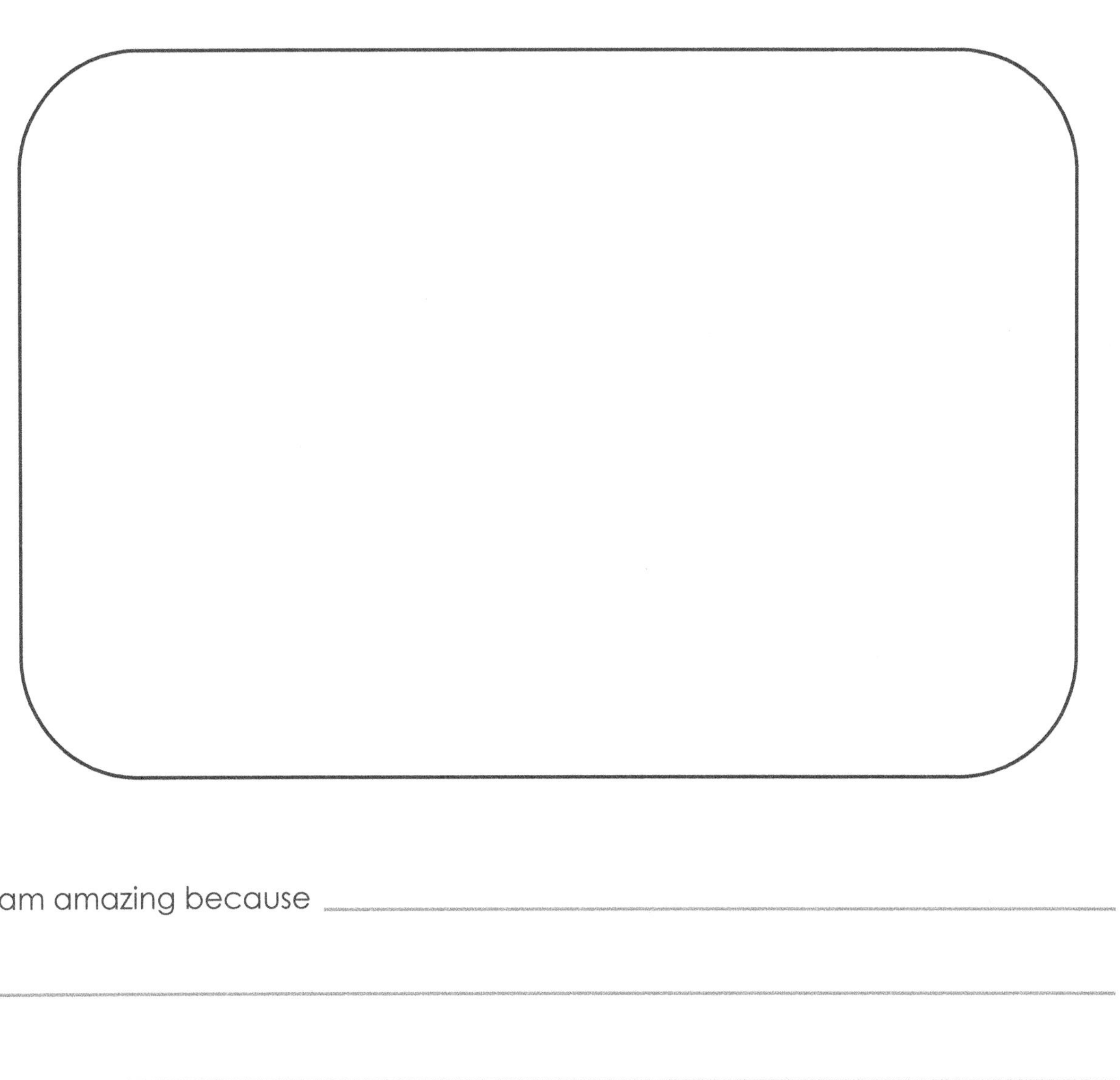

I am amazing because _______________________________

____

____

My Favorites

My favorite food is ____

My favorite color is ____

My favorite thing to do is _____________________________________

Draw your favorite thing.

I Can Help Myself Feel Better

When I feel sad, upset, or frustrated, I can...

Write, draw, or use a sticker to show what helps you feel better.

I Can Do Hard Things

Something I learned to do:

____

____

Write, draw, or use a sticker that shows how you felt.

I didn't give up!

Color Lyric being her amazing self.

I Kept Going!

Something that was hard, but I kept trying:

____

____

What helped me keep going?

____

____

Draw yourself not giving up.

Kind Words About Me

These are kind words I can say about myself:

I am helpful.

I am thoughtful.

I am nice.

Say these words out loud.
You may trace them if you want.
How do they make you feel?

____

One more kind word about me is

____

You may add a sticker that reminds you of how special you are.

My Superpower

My superpower is

____

Draw yourself using your superpower.

⭐ *Share your superpower with someone you trust.*

Something That Made Me Proud

Something I did that made me proud was

____

____

Draw that moment.

⭐ *Tell someone why you feel proud.*

Something I Do Well

One thing I do well is ______________________________

I am learning to ______________________________

Draw yourself doing something well.

When I Feel Good

What makes you feel happy?

____

____

____

Show what makes you happy! Write, draw, or use a sticker.

I Can Do Hard Things

Something I learned to do:

____

____

Write, draw, or use a sticker that shows how you felt.

I didn't give up!

Color and relax.

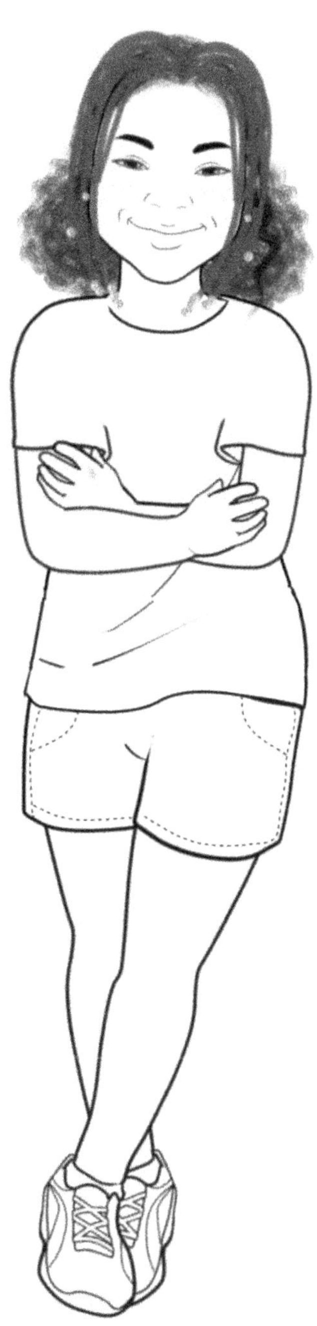

I Am Growing!

Something I'm getting better at:

____

____

Each step shows how you are growing. Draw yourself on the top step to celebrate how far you've come.

You may add a sticker that shows how you feel as you grow.

Kind Words About Me

These are kind words I can say about myself:

I am trying.

I am learning.

I am growing.

Say these words out loud.
You may trace them if you want.
How do they make you feel?

____

One more kind word about me is

____

You may add a sticker that reminds you of how special you are.

My Superpower

My superpower is

____

Draw yourself using your superpower.

I Am Amazing Because...

Write, draw, or use a sticker that shows what makes you amazing.

I am amazing because ______________________________________

____

____

My Feelings Today

Today I feel ____

When I feel this way, I like to _______________________________

____

____

Write, draw, or use a sticker to show how you feel.

I Can Help Myself Feel Better

When I feel sad, upset, or frustrated, I can...

Write, draw, or use a sticker to show what helps you feel better.

I Kept Going!

Something that was hard, but I kept trying:

____

____

What helped me keep going?

____

____

Draw yourself not giving up.

I Am Growing!

Something I'm getting better at:

____

____

Each step shows how you are growing. Draw yourself on the top step to celebrate how far you've come.

You may add a sticker that shows how you feel as you grow.

Kind Words About Me

These are kind words I can say about myself:

I am a good friend.

I am kind to others.

I am a good listener.

Say these words out loud.
You may trace them if you want.
How do they make you feel?

____

One more kind word about me is

____

You may add a sticker that reminds you of how special you are.

Something That Made Me Proud

Something I did that made me proud was

____

____

Draw that moment.

⭐ *Tell someone why you feel proud.*

I Am Amazing Because...

Write, draw, or use a sticker that shows what makes you amazing.

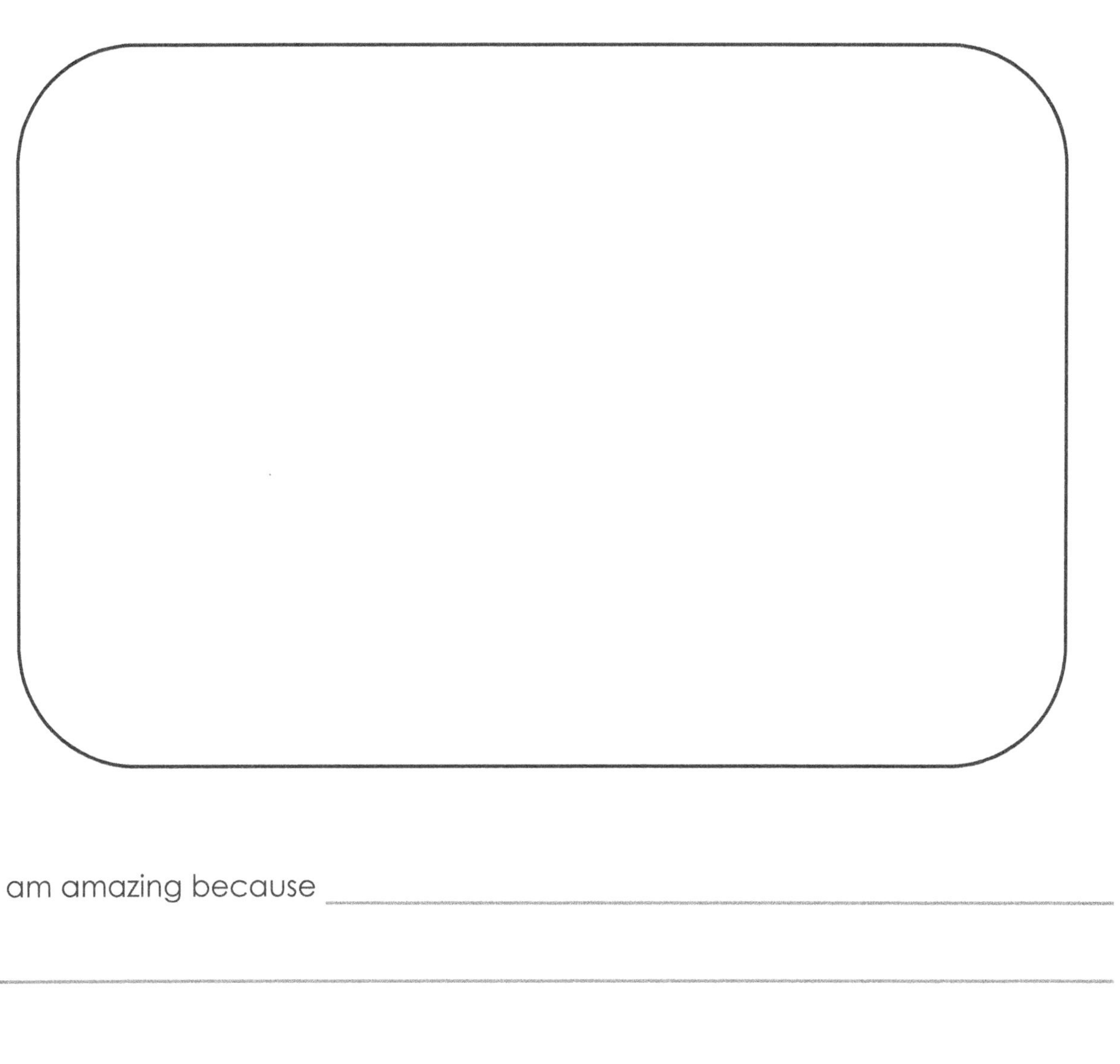

I am amazing because _______________________________________

____

____

What Makes Me, Me

Something special about me is ___________________________

____

____

Something I like about myself is ___________________________

____

____

Draw yourself.

When I Feel Good

What makes you feel happy?

Show what makes you happy! Write, draw, or use a sticker.

I Can Do Hard Things

Something I learned to do:

____

____

Write, draw, or use a sticker that shows how you felt.

I didn't give up!

Take a quiet moment and color Lyric.

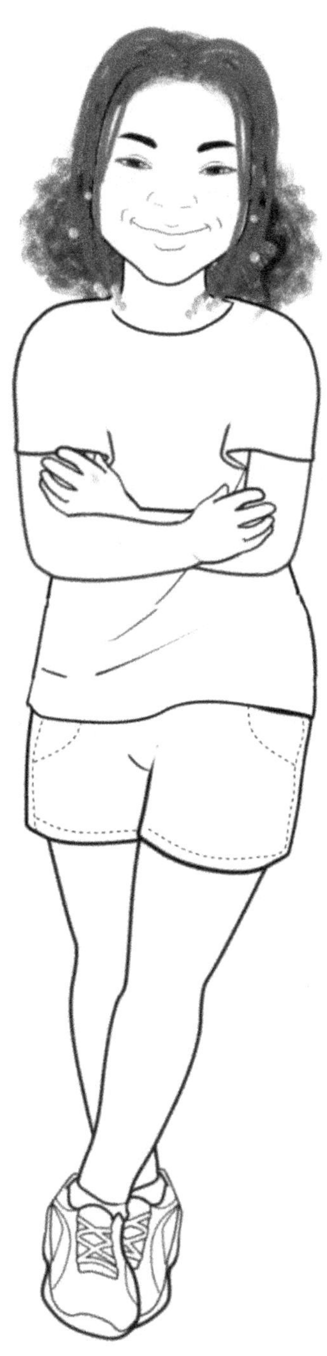

I Can Encourage Myself

When I need encouragement, I can say

"I can ____"

"I will ____"

"I am ____"

When I need encouragement, I can:

- ☐ Take a deep breath
- ☐ Ask for help
- ☐ Try again
- ☐ Take a break
- ☐ Think of something I did well
- ☐ Tell myself, "I can do this!"

Circle **all** that help you feel better.

Write, draw, or use a sticker to show how you encourage yourself.

★ *Tell someone what helps you keep going.*

Kind Words About Me

These are kind words I can say about myself:

I am enough.

I matter.

I am loved.

Say these words out loud.
You may trace them if you want.
How do they make you feel?

One more kind word about me is

You may add a sticker that reminds you of how special you are.

My Feelings Today

Today I feel ____

When I feel this way, I like to ______________________________

____

____

Write, draw, or use a sticker to show how you feel.

You Are Amazing!

Draw yourself doing something amazing.

This is me being amazing because

⭐ *Show this page to someone who loves you.*

Take a Moment

Write, draw, or use a sticker.

Something I want to remember is...

★ *Share something you want to remember.*

Write, draw, or create anything you want here.

Your ideas matter.

I am amazing—just being me!

When I Need Encouragement

Write, draw, or use a sticker to show what you say to yourself when things feel hard.

⭐ *Tell someone what you say to yourself when things feel hard.*

Share Your Words with Us

We'd love to see how you're using your journal!

With help from a parent or teacher, you can:

- Share a favorite page
- Show a drawing or reflection
- Tell us what you learned

Your voice matters. We'd love to celebrate your ideas!

Tag us @PenOfTheWriter

or share with #WhenISeeMe

Scan the code below to post in our Facebook group.

WhenISeeMe.com

Your words matter.

You are important.

Your voice matters.

Your story matters.